W9-BCR-593

# SURVIVING THE GREAT CHICAGO FIRE

By Jo Cleland
Illustrated By Pete McDonnell

ROURKE PUBLISHING

Vero Beach, Florida 32964

www.rourkepublishing.com

Photo Credits: © Tomograf: page 28

Edited by Meg Greve
Illustrated by Pete McDonnell
Art Direction and Page Layout by Renee Brady

**Library of Congress Cataloging-in-Publication Data**

Cleland, Joann.
Surviving the Great Chicago Fire / Jo Cleland.
    p. cm. -- (Eye on history graphic illustrated)
Includes bibliographical references and index.
ISBN 978-1-60694-440-0 (alk. paper)
ISBN 978-1-60694-549-0 (soft cover)
1.  Great Fire, Chicago, Ill., 1871--Juvenile literature. 2.  Fires--Illinois--Chicago--History--19th century--Juvenile literature. 3.  Chicago (Ill.)--History--To 1875--Juvenile literature. I. Title.
F548.42.C68 2010
977.3'11041--dc22
                                    2009020501

Printed in the USA
CG/CG

www.rourkepublishing.com - rourke@rourkepublishing.com
Post Office Box 643328  Vero Beach, Florida 32964

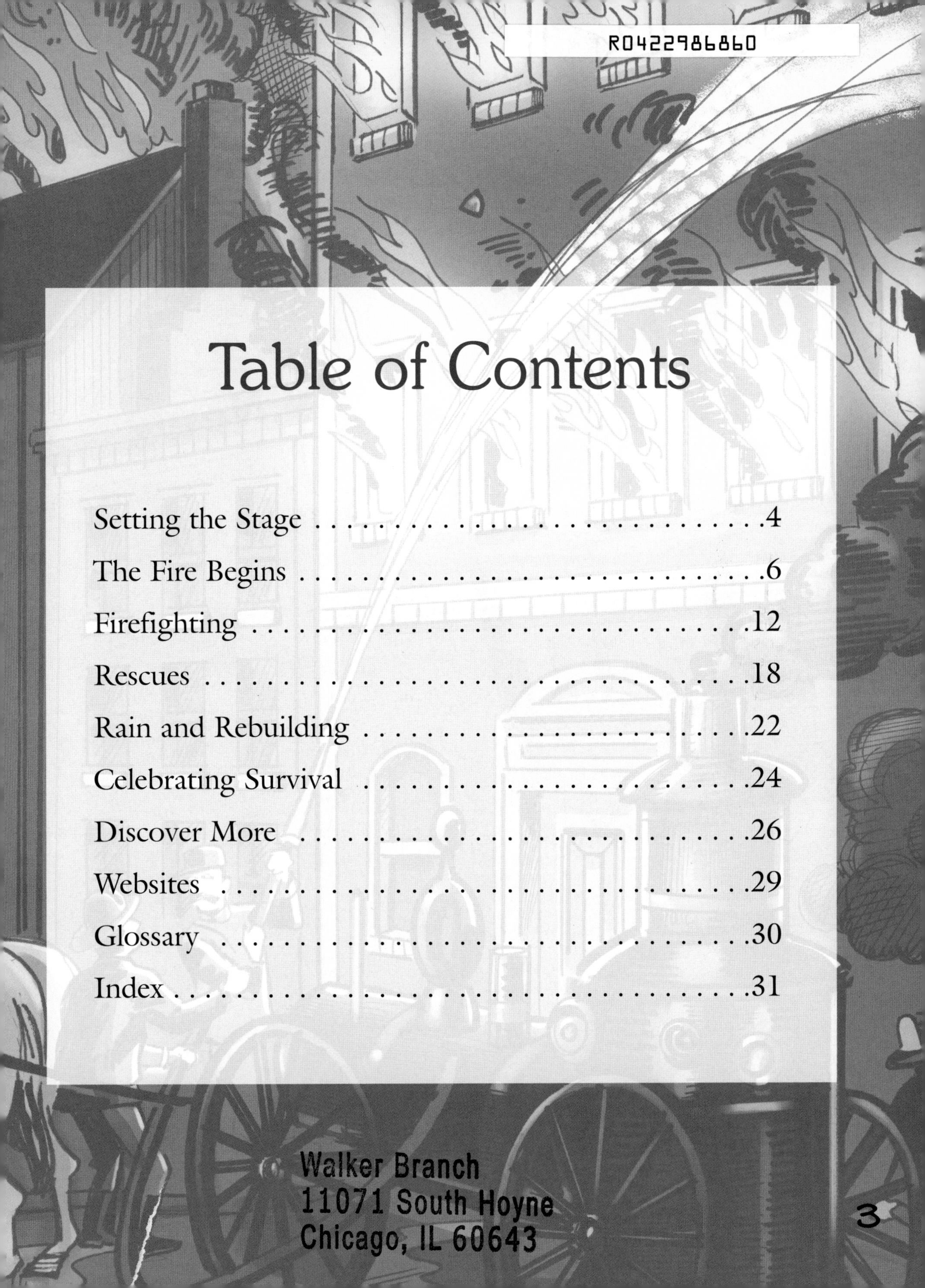

# Table of Contents

Setting the Stage . . . . . . . . . . . . . . . . . . . . . . . .4

The Fire Begins . . . . . . . . . . . . . . . . . . . . . . . . .6

Firefighting . . . . . . . . . . . . . . . . . . . . . . . . . . .12

Rescues . . . . . . . . . . . . . . . . . . . . . . . . . . . . .18

Rain and Rebuilding . . . . . . . . . . . . . . . . . . . .22

Celebrating Survival . . . . . . . . . . . . . . . . . . . .24

Discover More . . . . . . . . . . . . . . . . . . . . . . . .26

Websites . . . . . . . . . . . . . . . . . . . . . . . . . . . .29

Glossary . . . . . . . . . . . . . . . . . . . . . . . . . . . .30

Index . . . . . . . . . . . . . . . . . . . . . . . . . . . . . .31

# Chicago Daily News

Thursday

Issue 7  Volume 11

October 12, 1871

## Fire Destroys Four Square Miles

On Sunday, October 8, people in downtown Chicago awoke to see flames leaping at their homes. Grabbing anything they could, they fled toward Lake Michigan. Hundreds did not escape in time, and many suffered serious burns. All lost their homes.

Rumor has it, Mrs. O'Leary's cow kicked over a lantern in her barn, starting this disaster. However, the story has not been confirmed. What is known is that fire totally destroyed four square miles. Wooden buildings fueled the fires moving across the area. The city is pulling together to aid those suffering great losses.

*One star on Chicago's official flag stands for the building of Fort Dearborn, the next star stands for the Great Chicago Fire, and the last two stand for the World's Fairs in 1893 and 1933. The top and bottom blue stripes represent Lake Michigan and the Chicago River.*

One of the largest fires of the 19th century burned for two days and destroyed four square miles (10 square kilometers) in Chicago. More than 300 people lost their lives, and 100,000 lost their homes.

Several different reasons for the start of the fire have been suggested. The most well-known is that it began when a cow kicked over a lantern in Mrs. O'Leary's barn. Regardless of the reason, Chicago was devasted by the fire. The citizens, however, were commited to rebuilding this great city. Within just four years, workers rebuilt what was lost. Chicago was better than ever.

# The Fire Begins

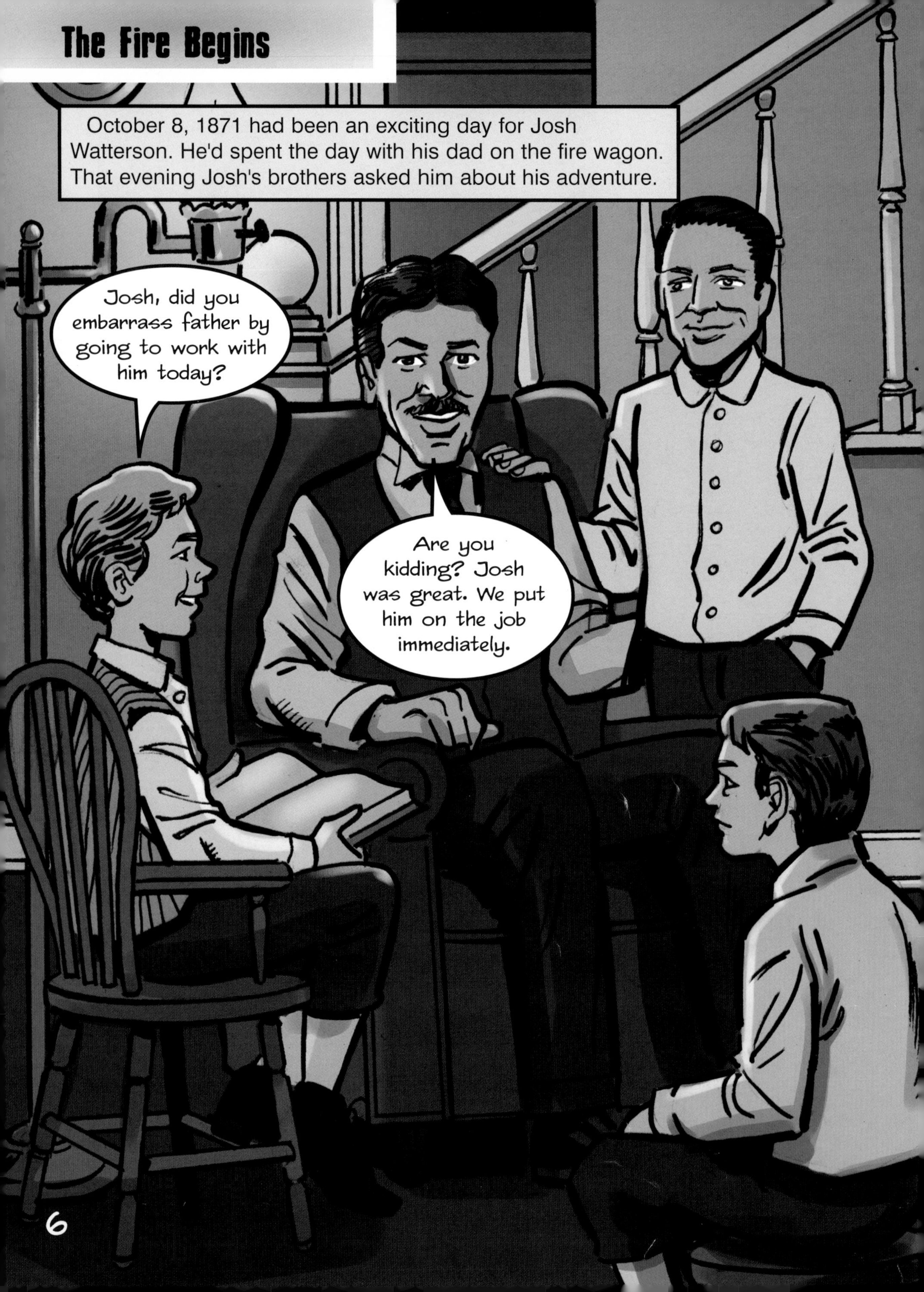

October 8, 1871 had been an exciting day for Josh Watterson. He'd spent the day with his dad on the fire wagon. That evening Josh's brothers asked him about his adventure.
Josh, did you embarrass father by going to work with him today?
Are you kidding? Josh was great. We put him on the job immediately.

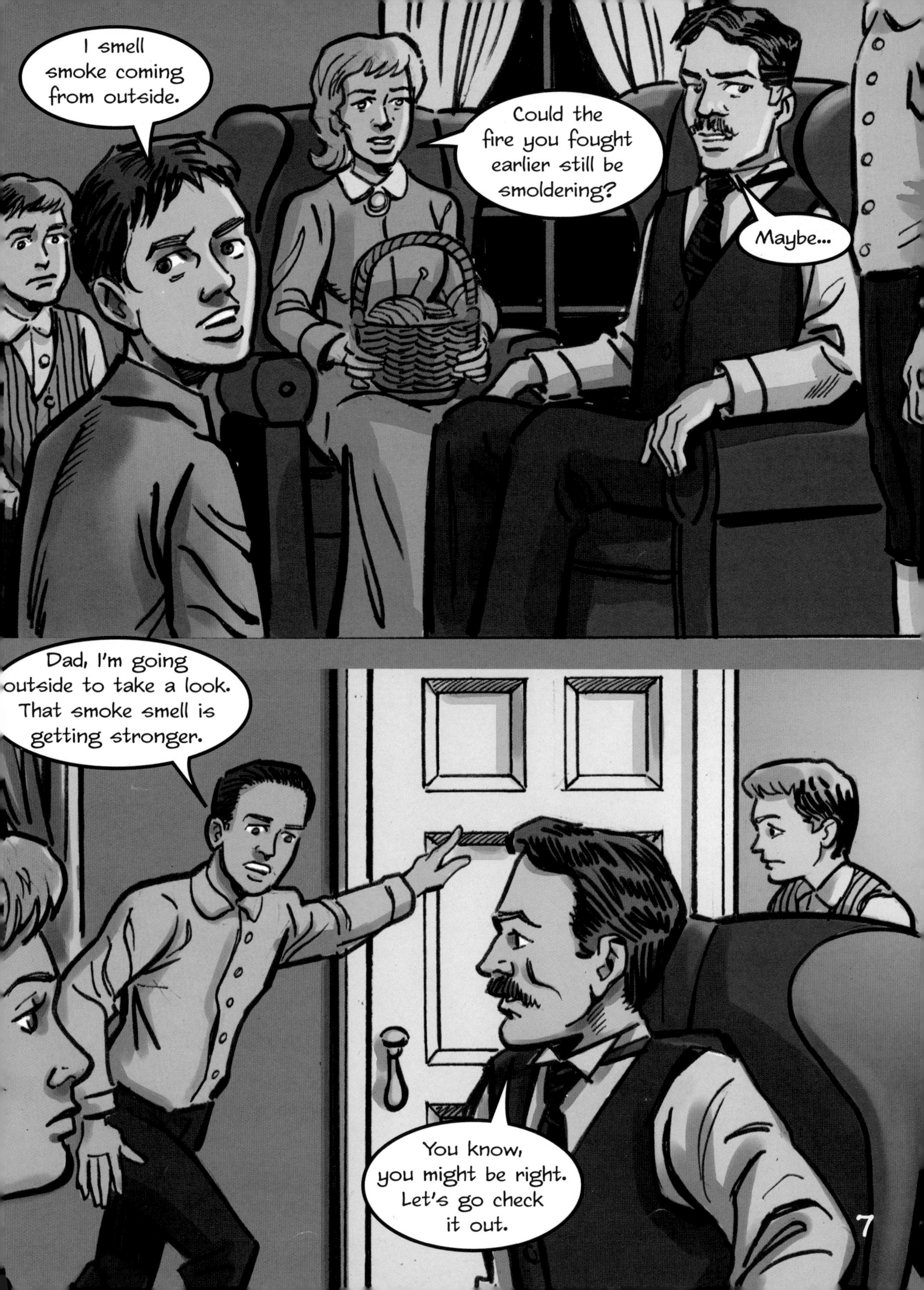
I smell smoke coming from outside.
Could the fire you fought earlier still be smoldering?
Maybe...
Dad, I'm going outside to take a look. That smoke smell is getting stronger.
You know, you might be right. Let's go check it out.

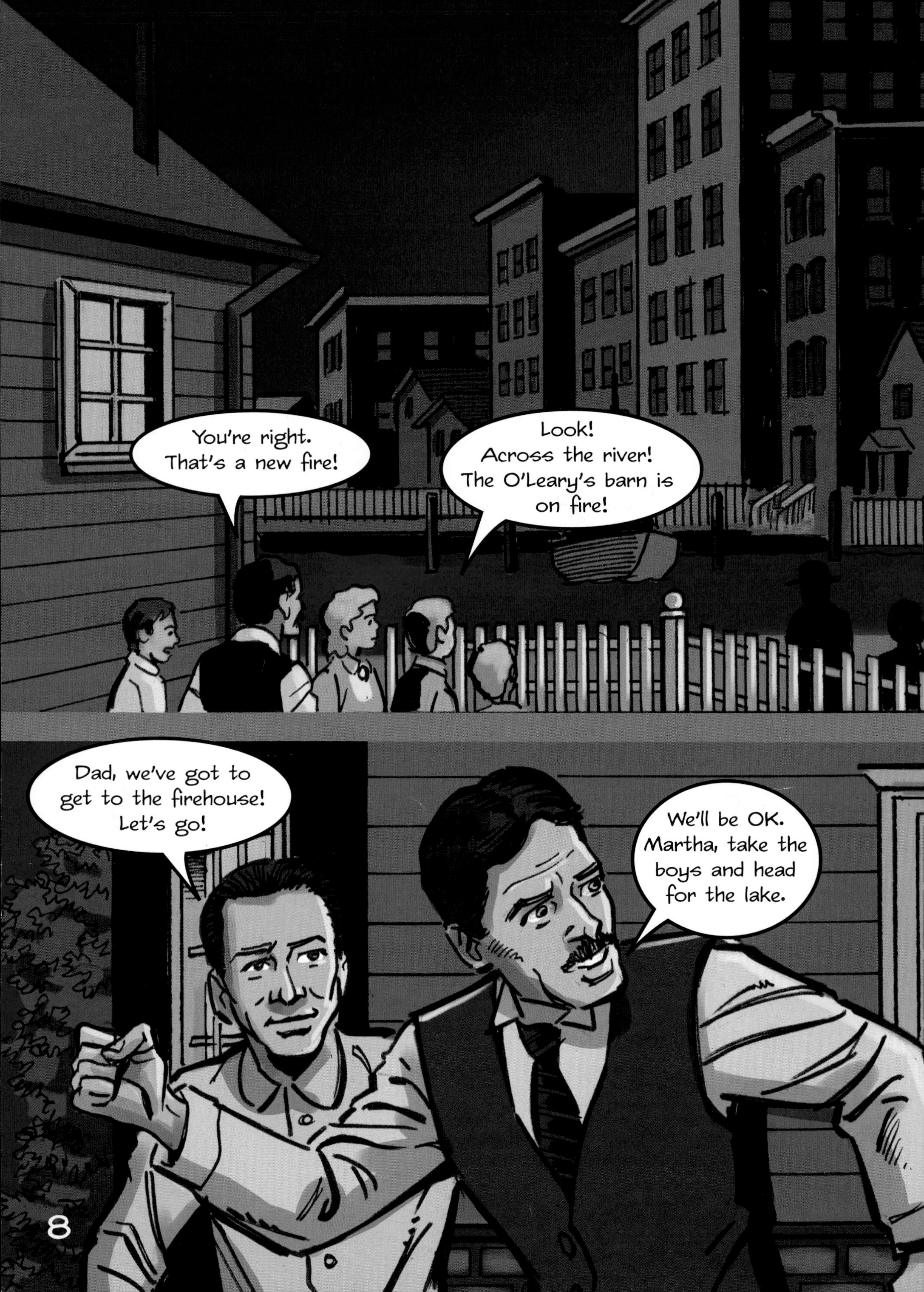
You're right. That's a new fire!
Look! Across the river! The O'Leary's barn is on fire!
Dad, we've got to get to the firehouse! Let's go!
We'll be OK. Martha, take the boys and head for the lake.

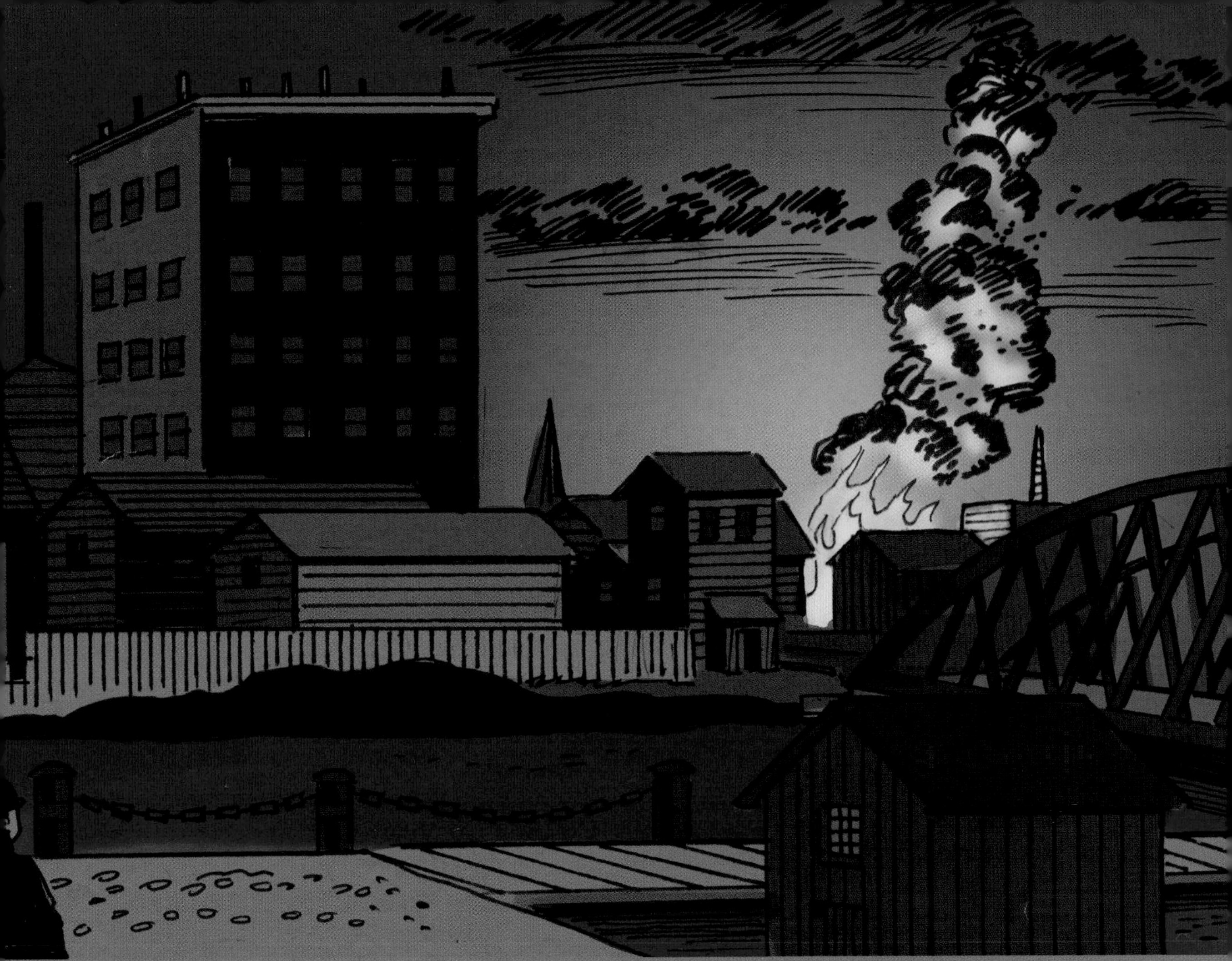

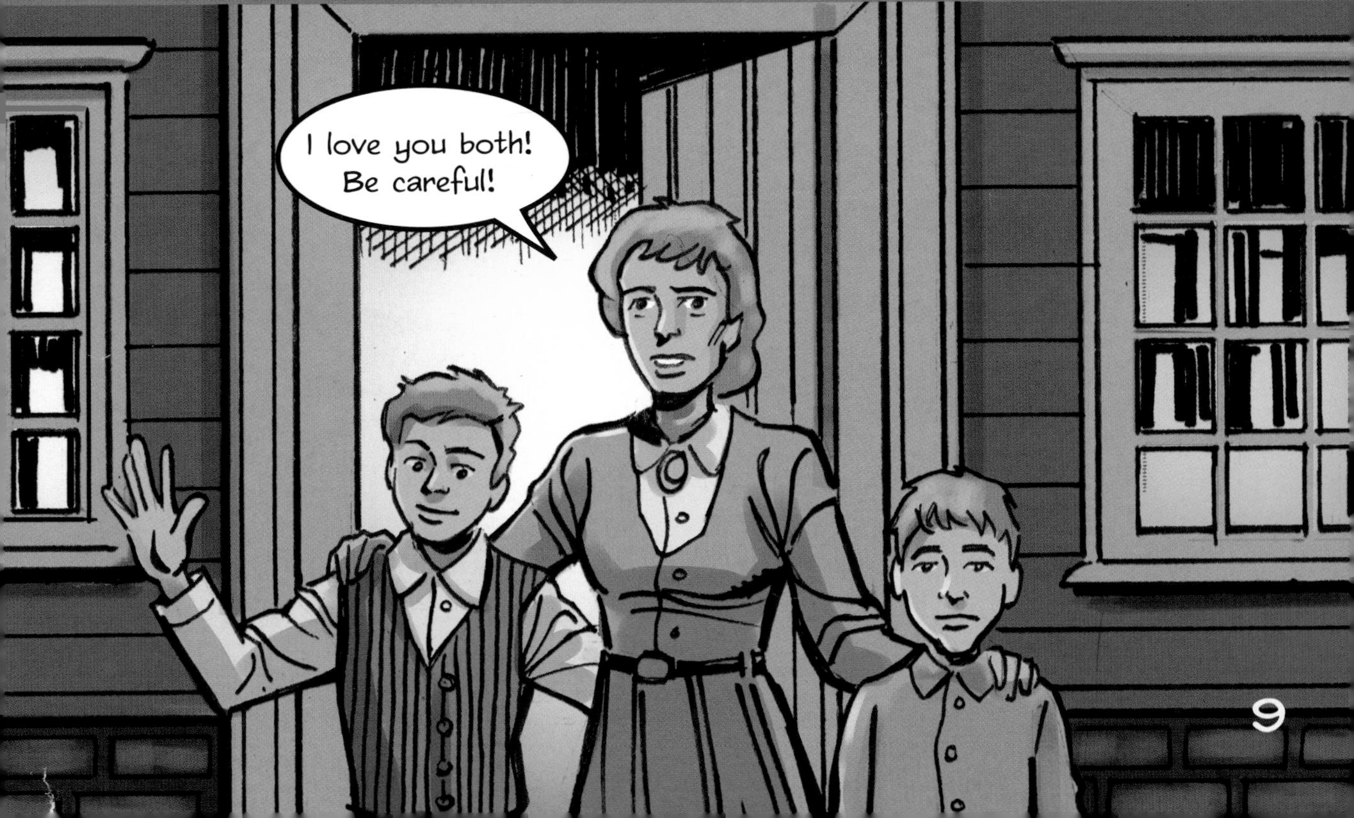
I love you both! Be careful!

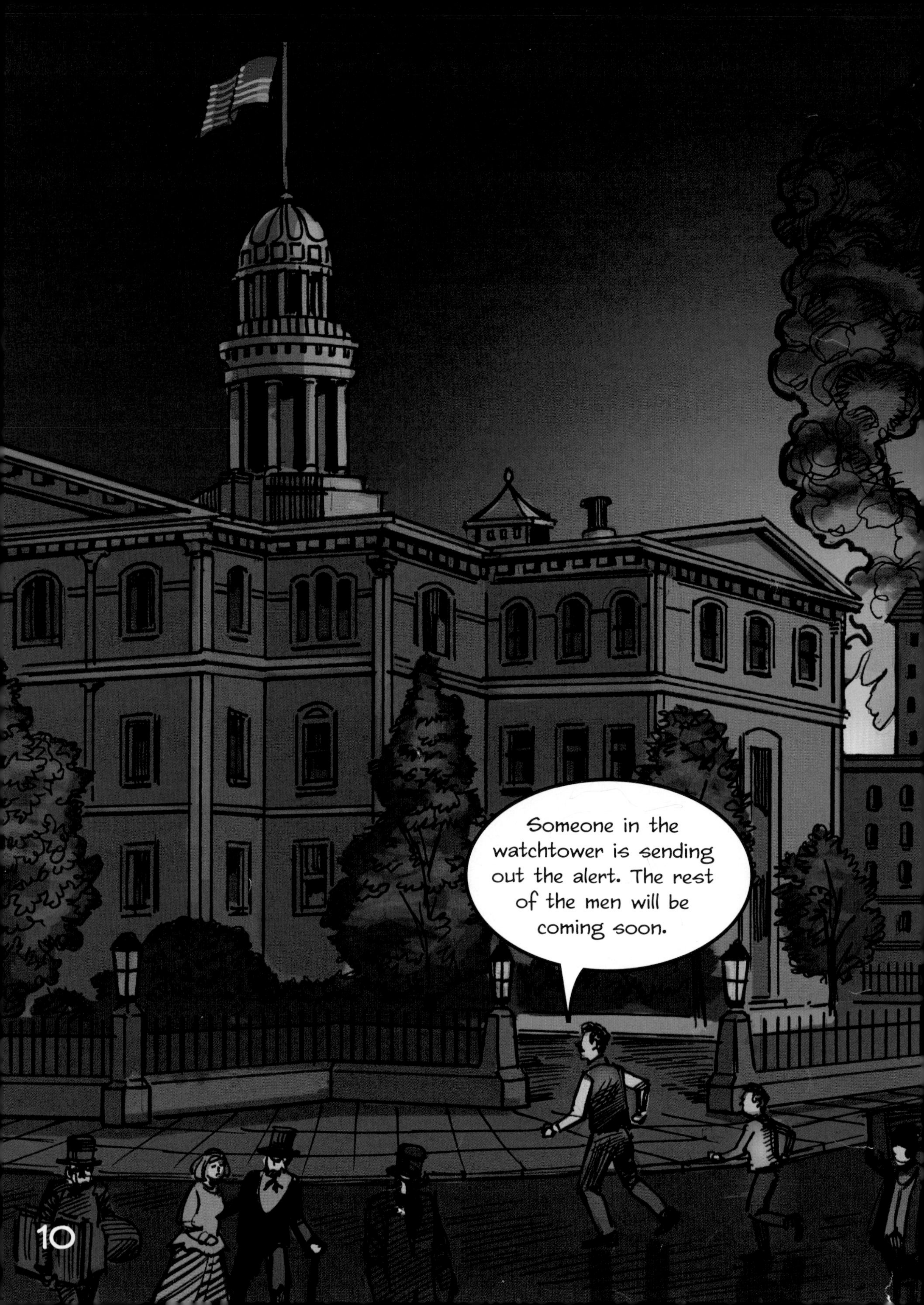
Someone in the watchtower is sending out the alert. The rest of the men will be coming soon.

As Josh and his dad rush on, a wind whips the fire into raging tongues of fire.

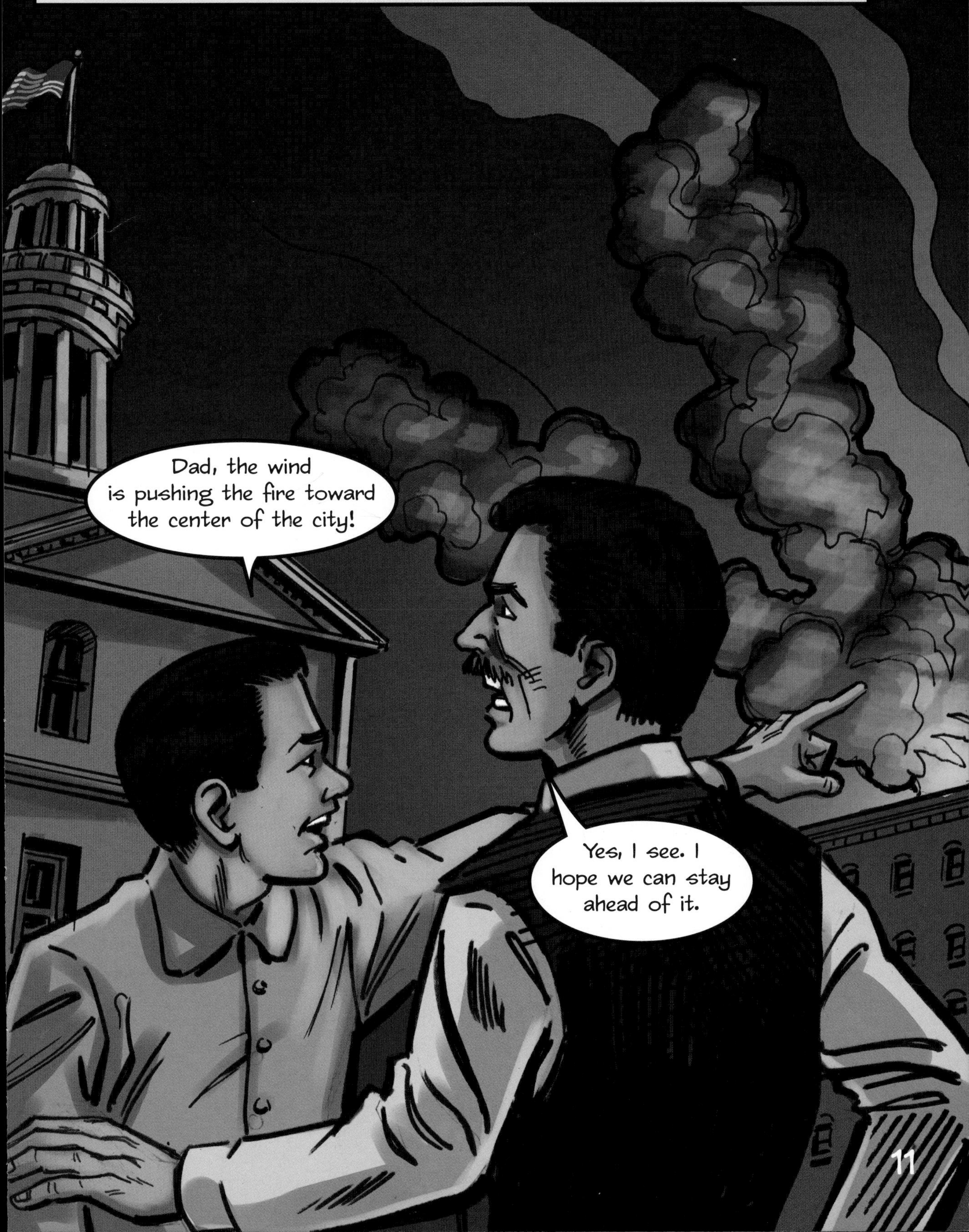
Dad, the wind is pushing the fire toward the center of the city!
Yes, I see. I hope we can stay ahead of it.

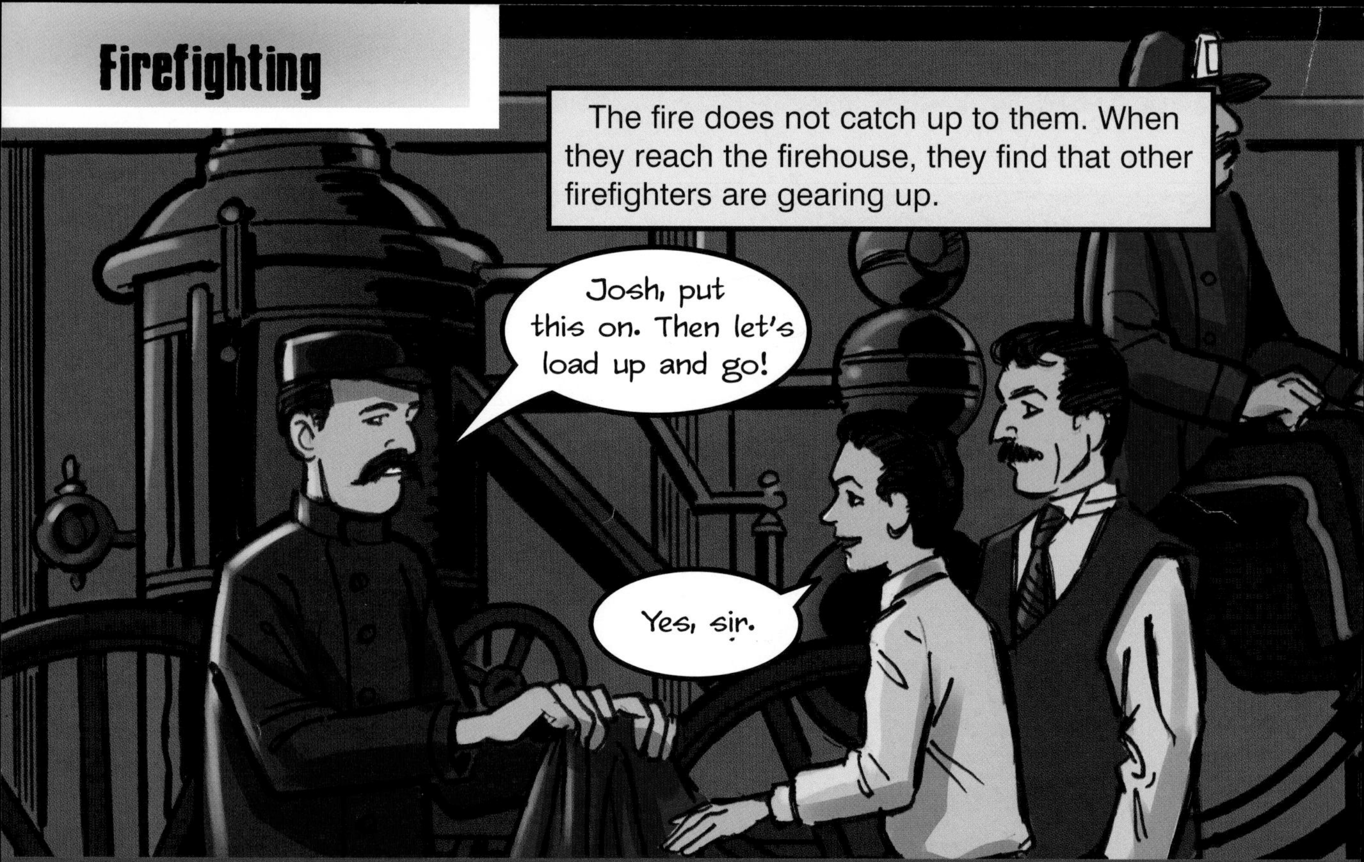
The fire does not catch up to them. When they reach the firehouse, they find that other firefighters are gearing up.
Josh, put this on. Then let's load up and go!
Yes, sir.

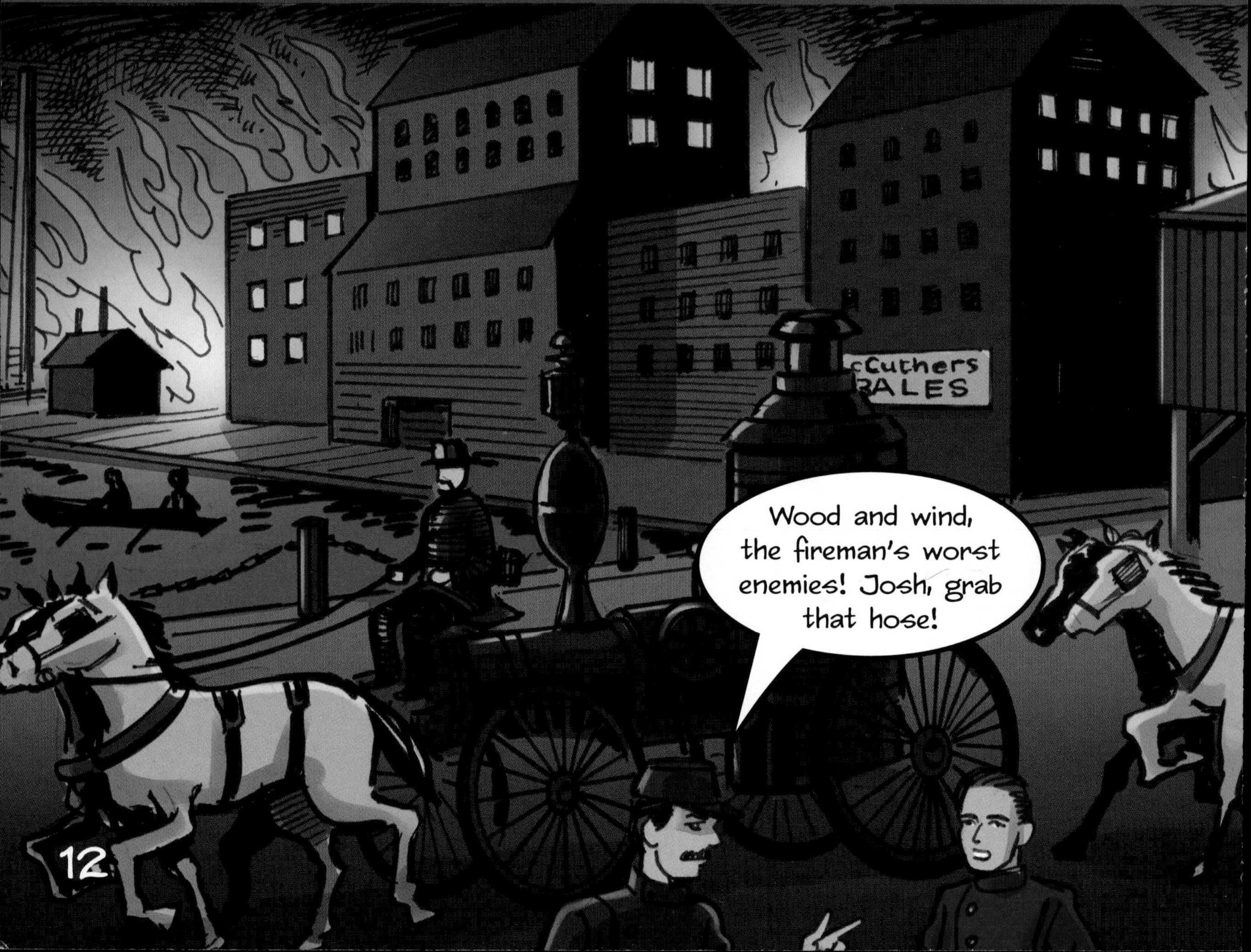
cCuthers
BALES
Wood and wind, the fireman's worst enemies! Josh, grab that hose!

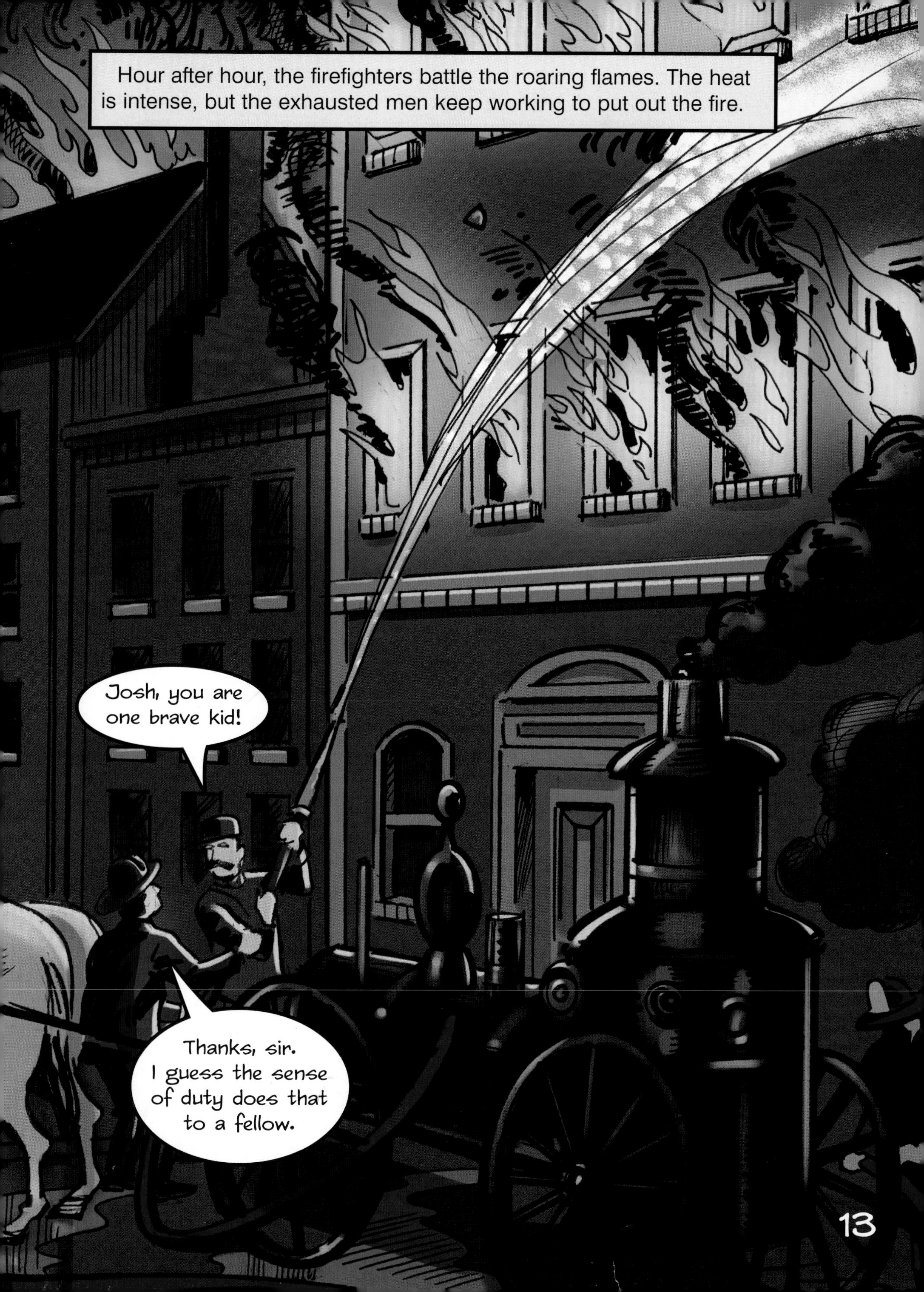
Hour after hour, the firefighters battle the roaring flames. The heat is intense, but the exhausted men keep working to put out the fire.
Josh, you are one brave kid!
Thanks, sir. I guess the sense of duty does that to a fellow.

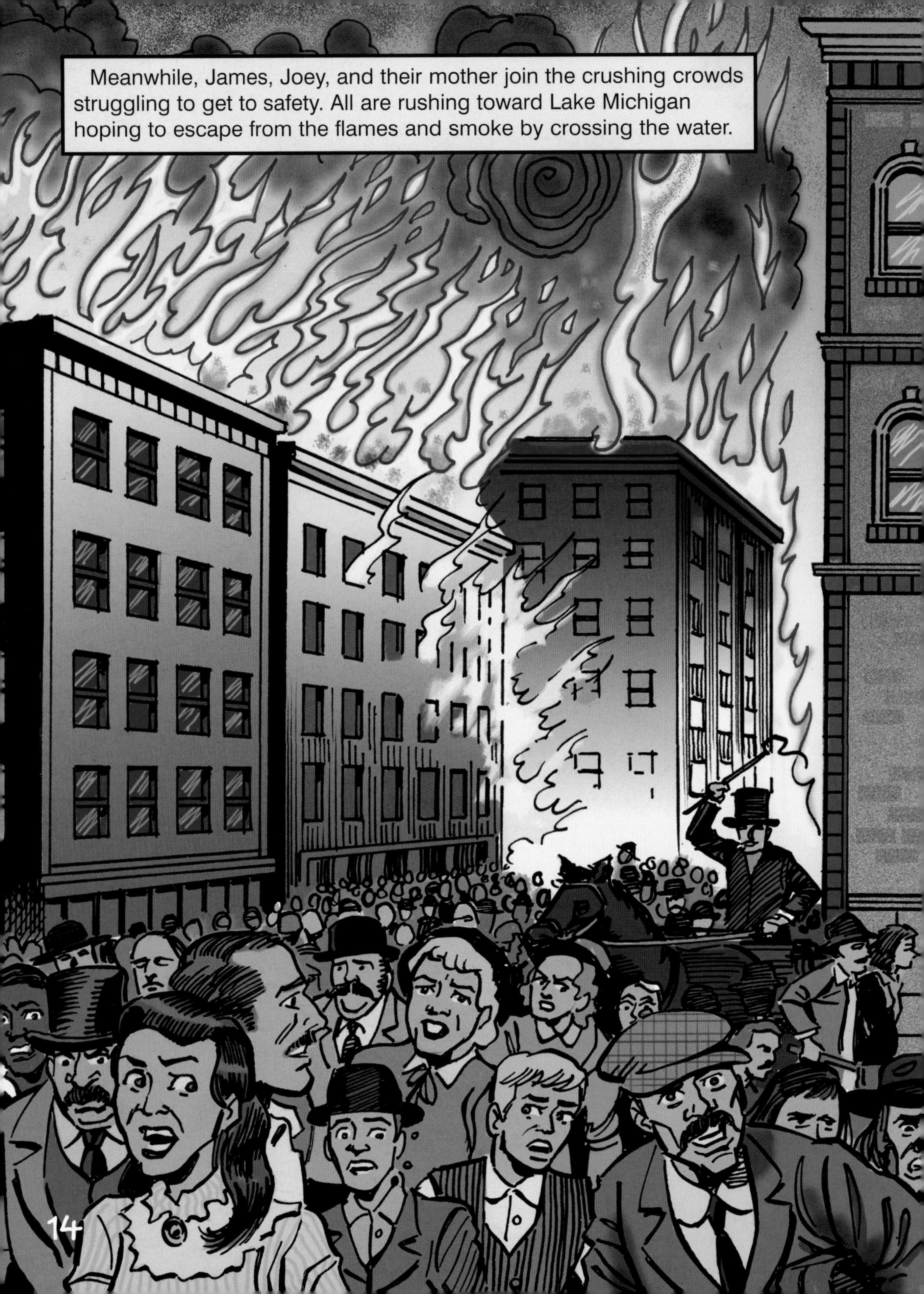
Meanwhile, James, Joey, and their mother join the crushing crowds struggling to get to safety. All are rushing toward Lake Michigan hoping to escape from the flames and smoke by crossing the water.

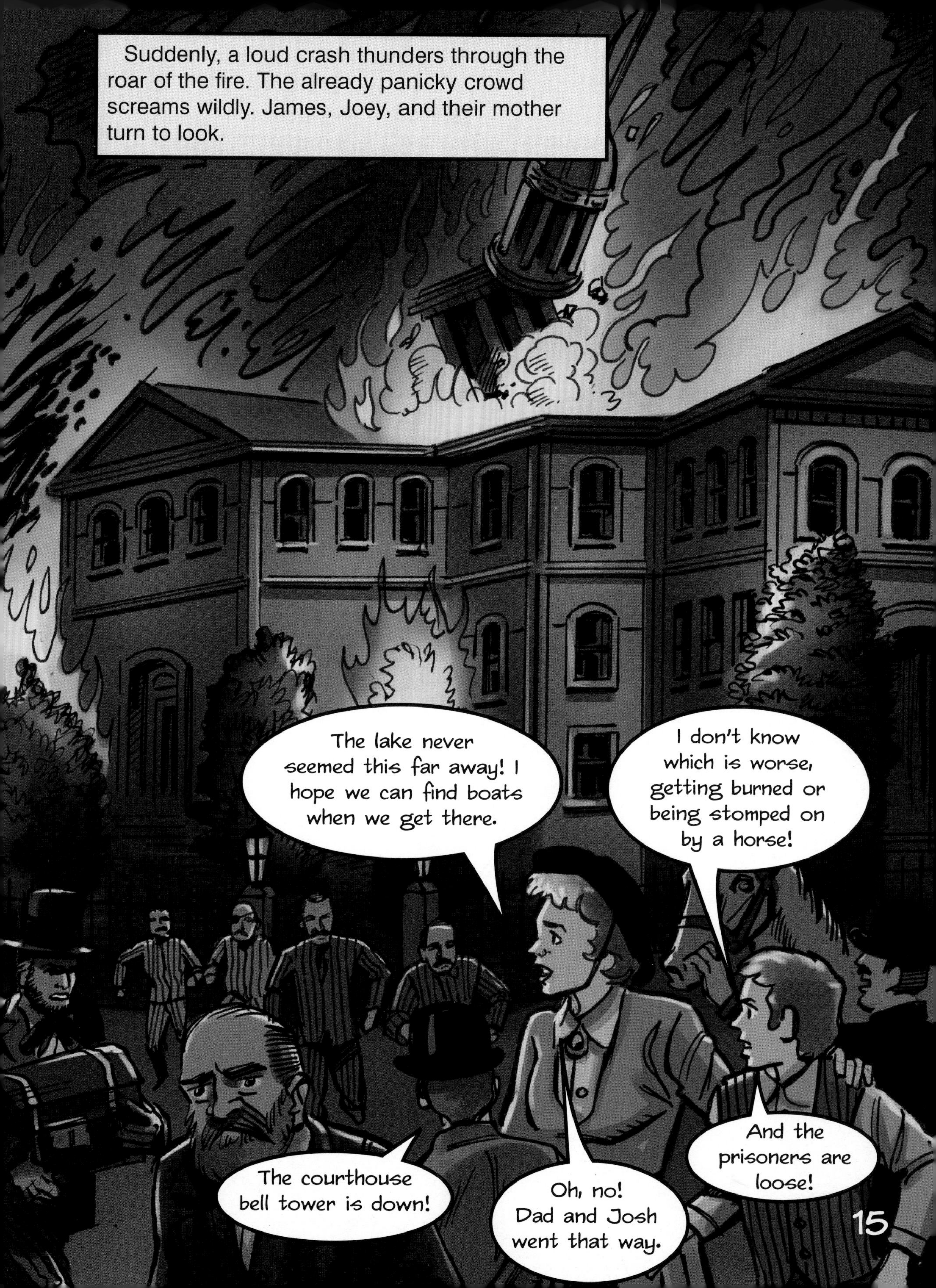
Suddenly, a loud crash thunders through the roar of the fire. The already panicky crowd screams wildly. James, Joey, and their mother turn to look.
The lake never seemed this far away! I hope we can find boats when we get there.
I don't know which is worse, getting burned or being stomped on by a horse!
The courthouse bell tower is down!
Oh, no! Dad and Josh went that way.
And the prisoners are loose!

Josh and his father are not harmed by the falling courthouse bell tower, nor by the escaped prisoners. But at 3:20 a.m., after nearly five hours of helping force back the flames, they face a new problem.

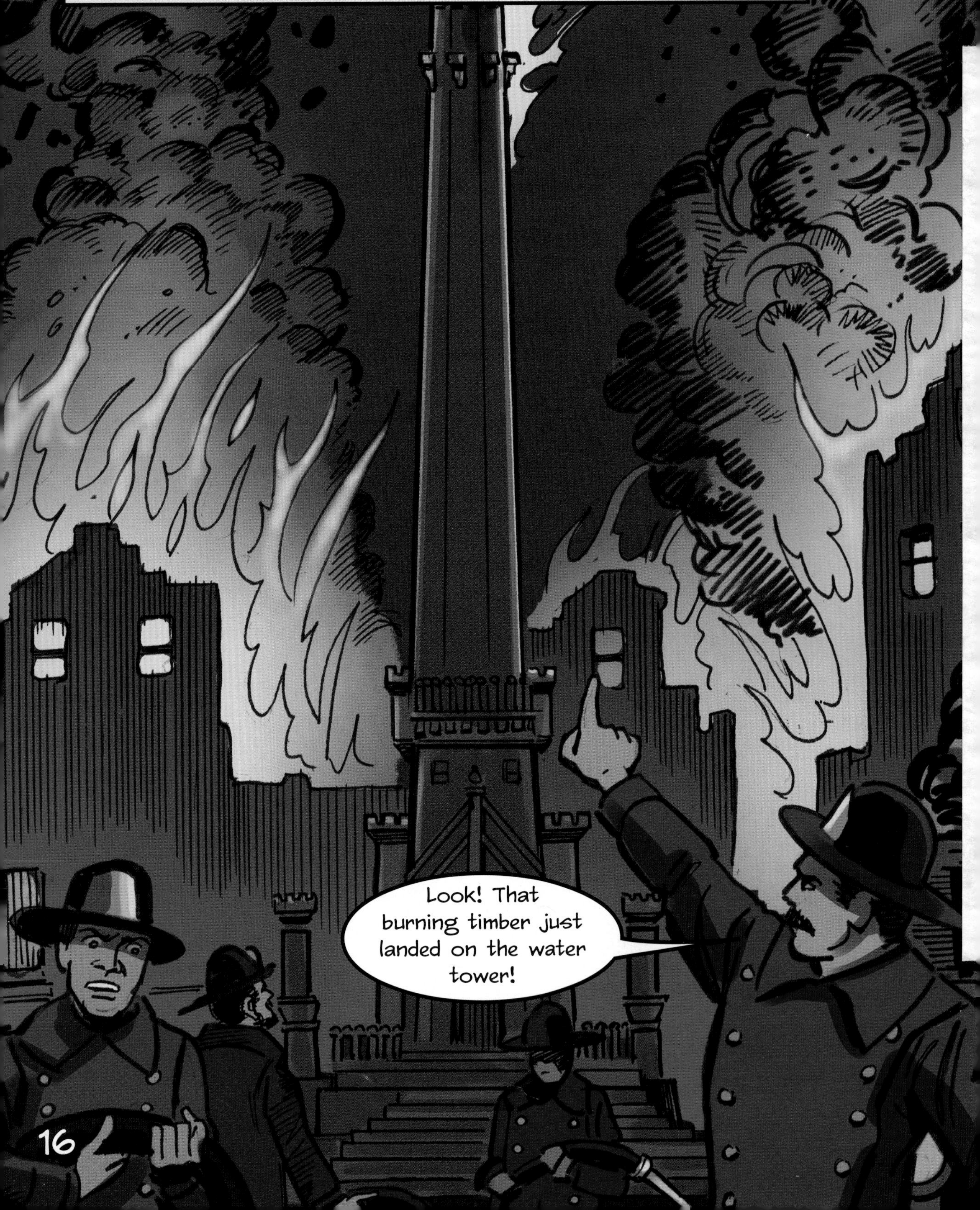
Look! That burning timber just landed on the water tower!

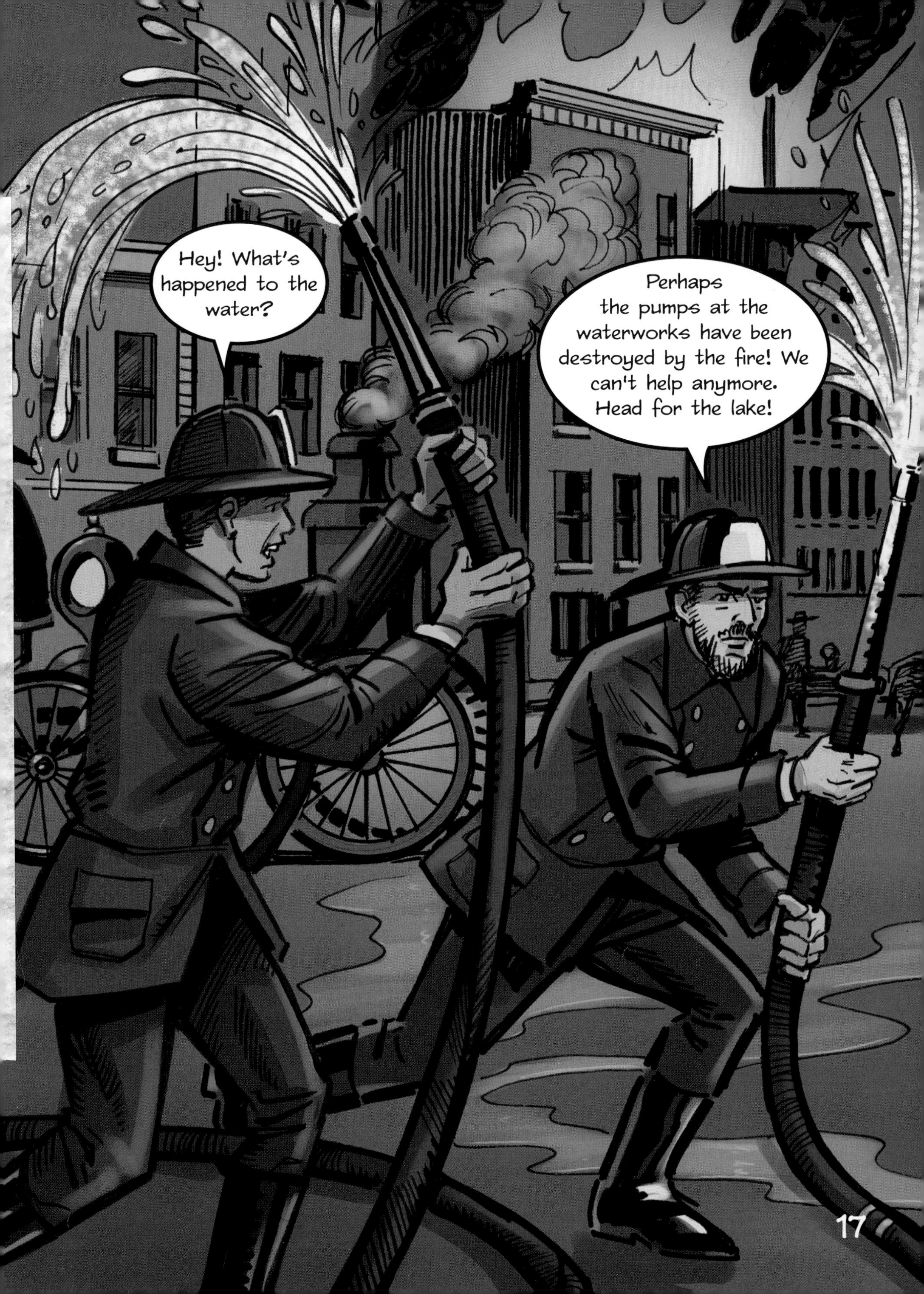
Hey! What's happened to the water?
Perhaps the pumps at the waterworks have been destroyed by the fire! We can't help anymore. Head for the lake!

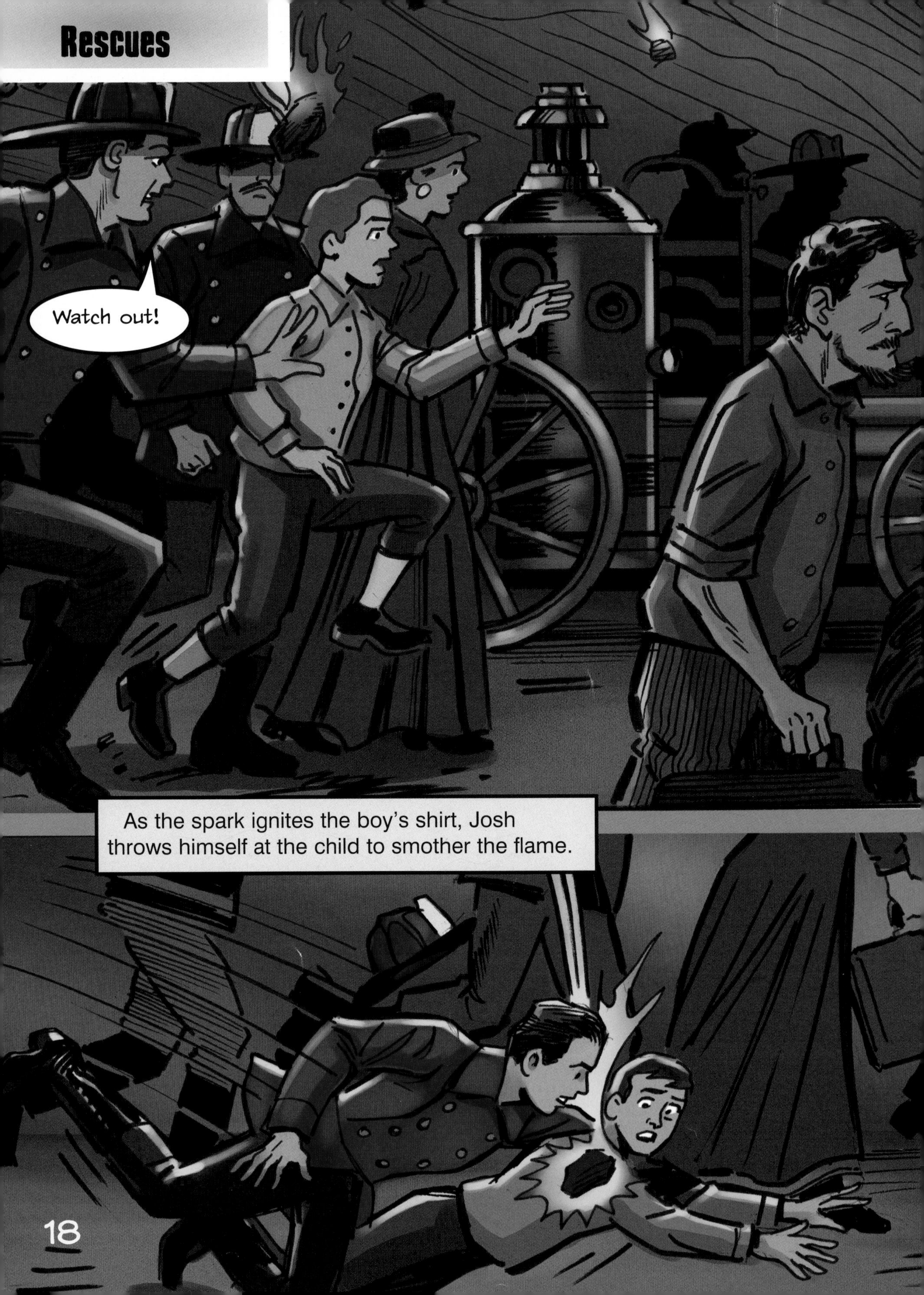
Watch out!
As the spark ignites the boy's shirt, Josh throws himself at the child to smother the flame.

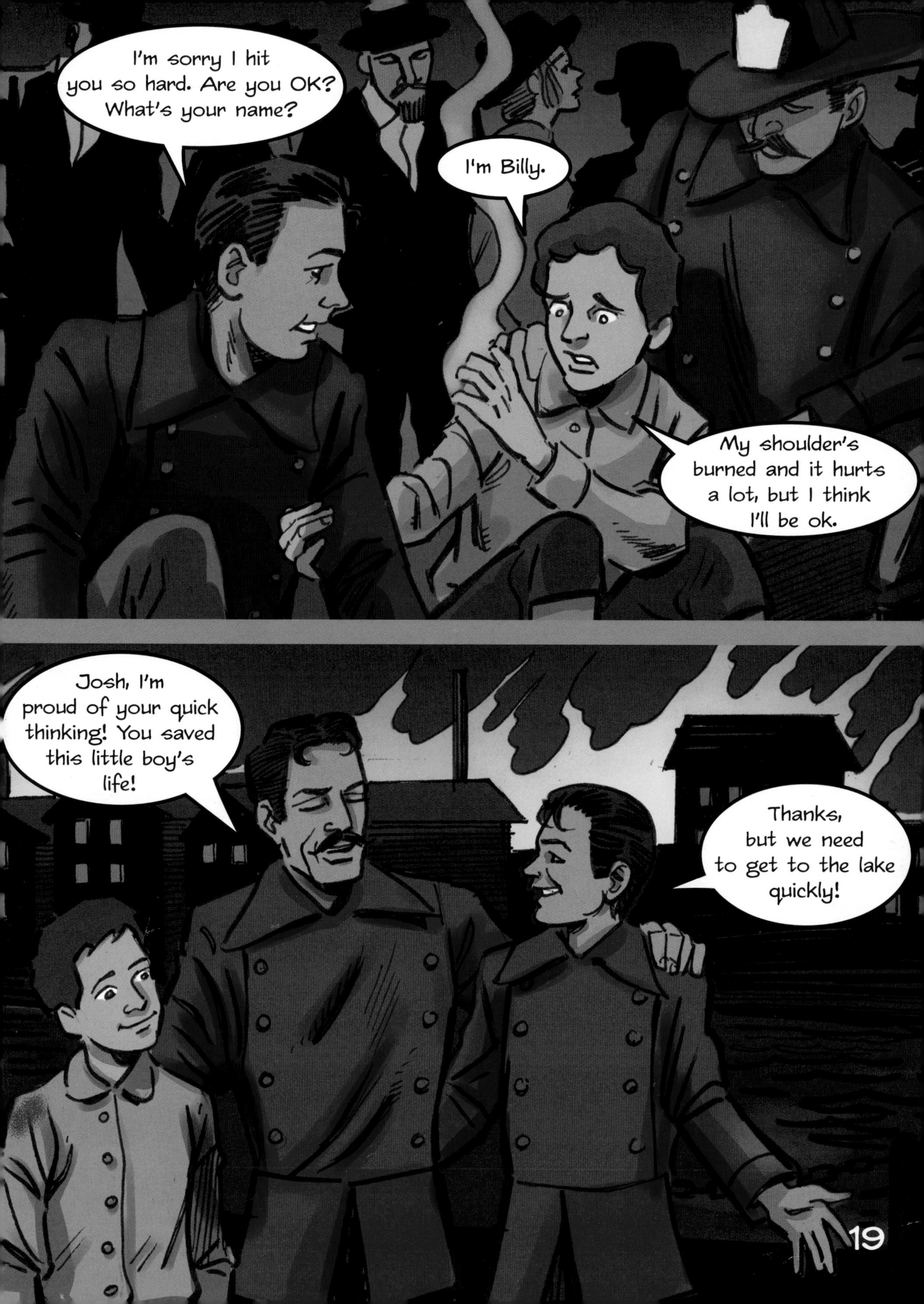
I'm sorry I hit you so hard. Are you OK? What's your name?
I'm Billy.
My shoulder's burned and it hurts a lot, but I think I'll be ok.
Josh, I'm proud of your quick thinking! You saved this little boy's life!
Thanks, but we need to get to the lake quickly!

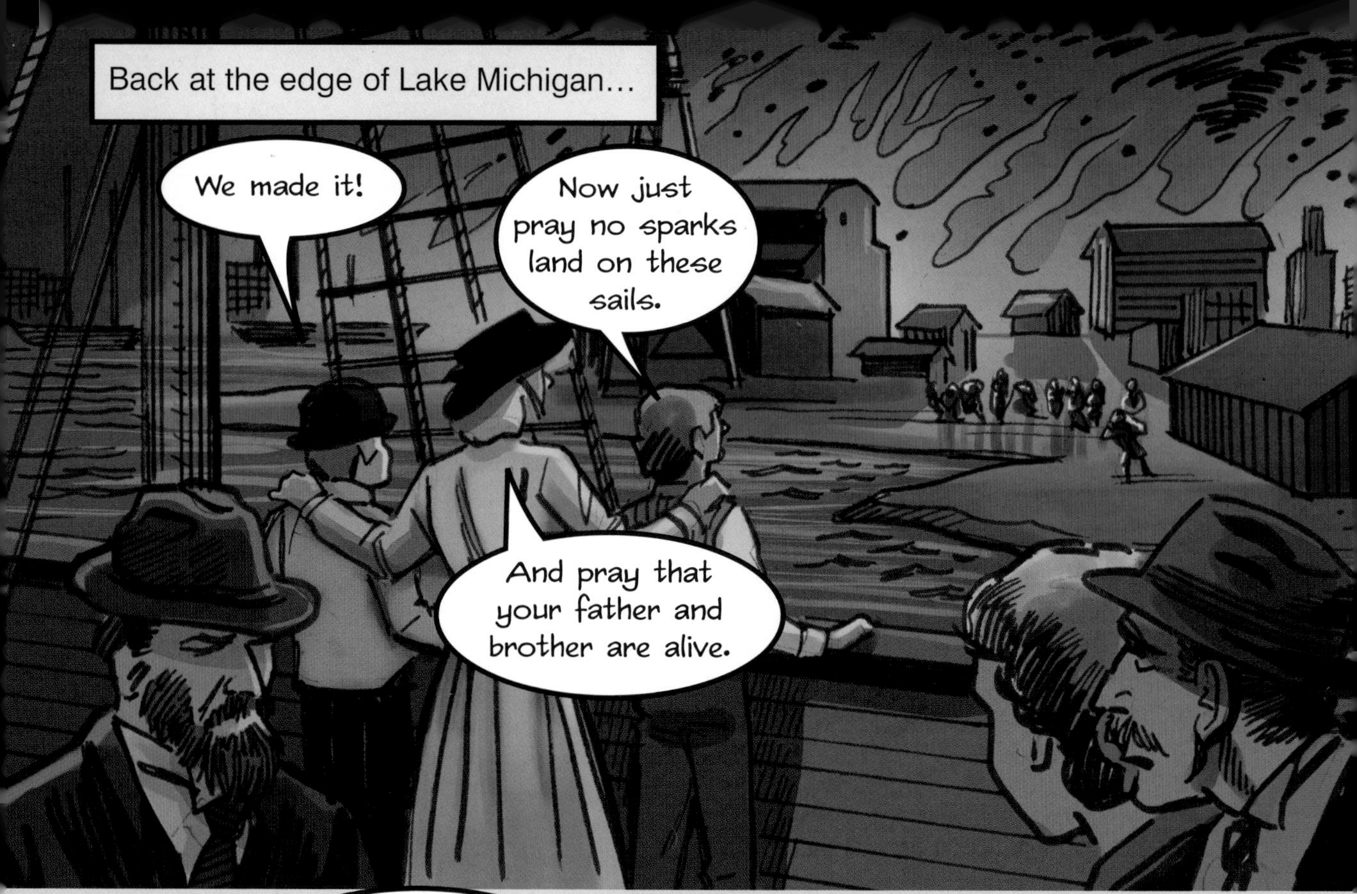
Back at the edge of Lake Michigan…
We made it!
Now just pray no sparks land on these sails.
And pray that your father and brother are alive.

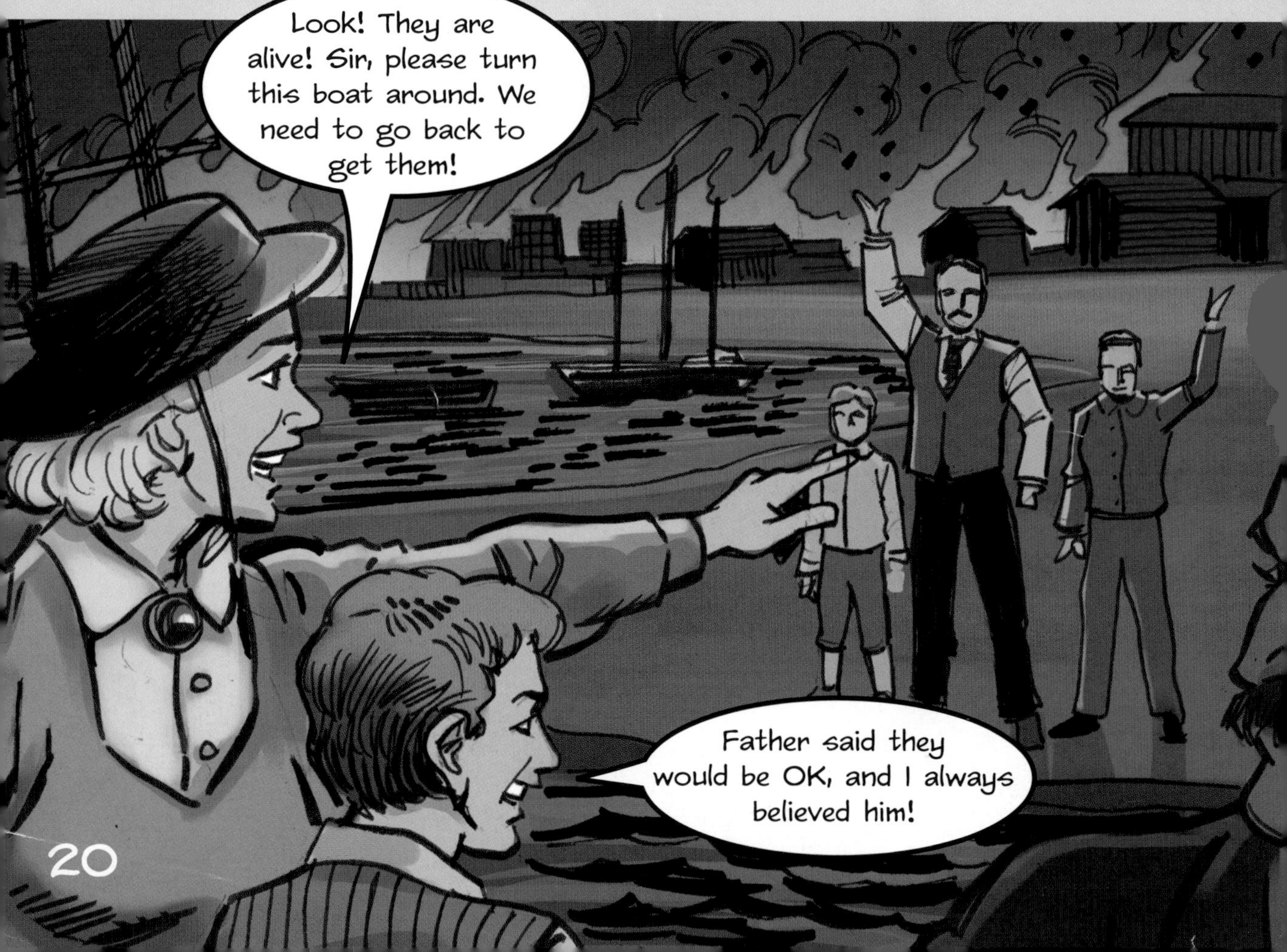
Look! They are alive! Sir, please turn this boat around. We need to go back to get them!
Father said they would be OK, and I always believed him!

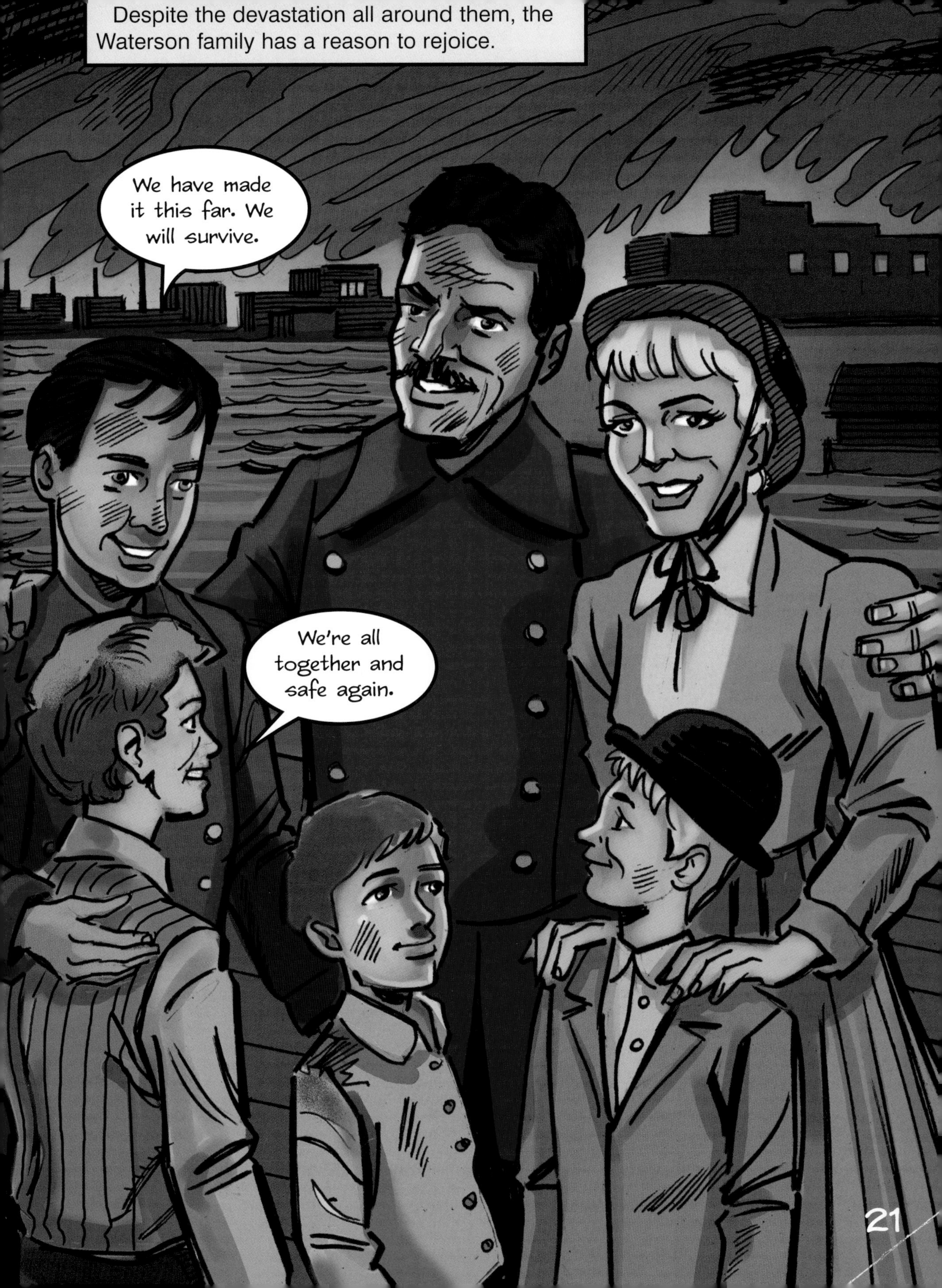
Despite the devastation all around them, the Waterson family has a reason to rejoice.
We have made it this far. We will survive.
We're all together and safe again.

# Rain and Rebuilding

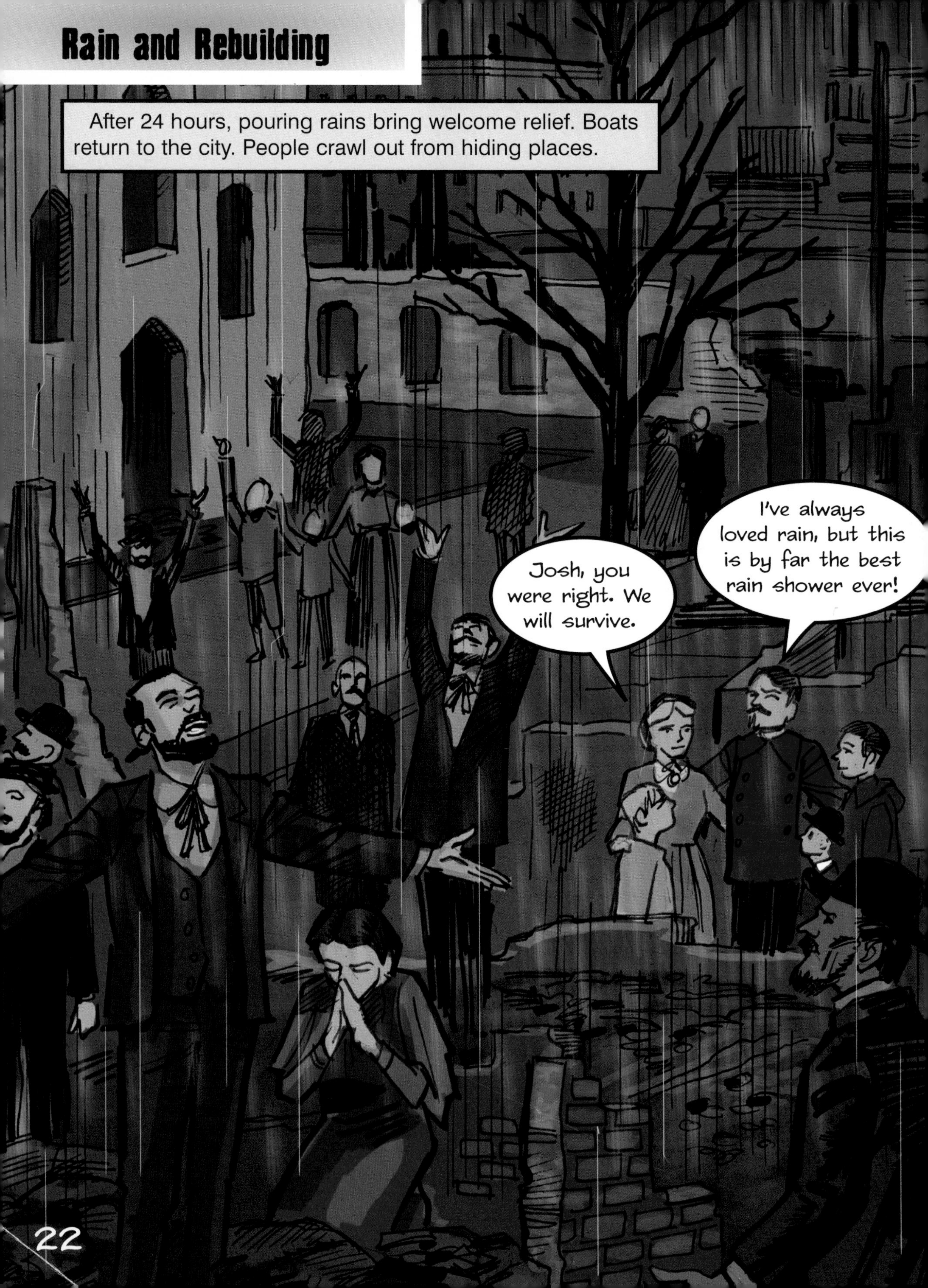
After 24 hours, pouring rains bring welcome relief. Boats return to the city. People crawl out from hiding places.
Josh, you were right. We will survive.
I've always loved rain, but this is by far the best rain shower ever!

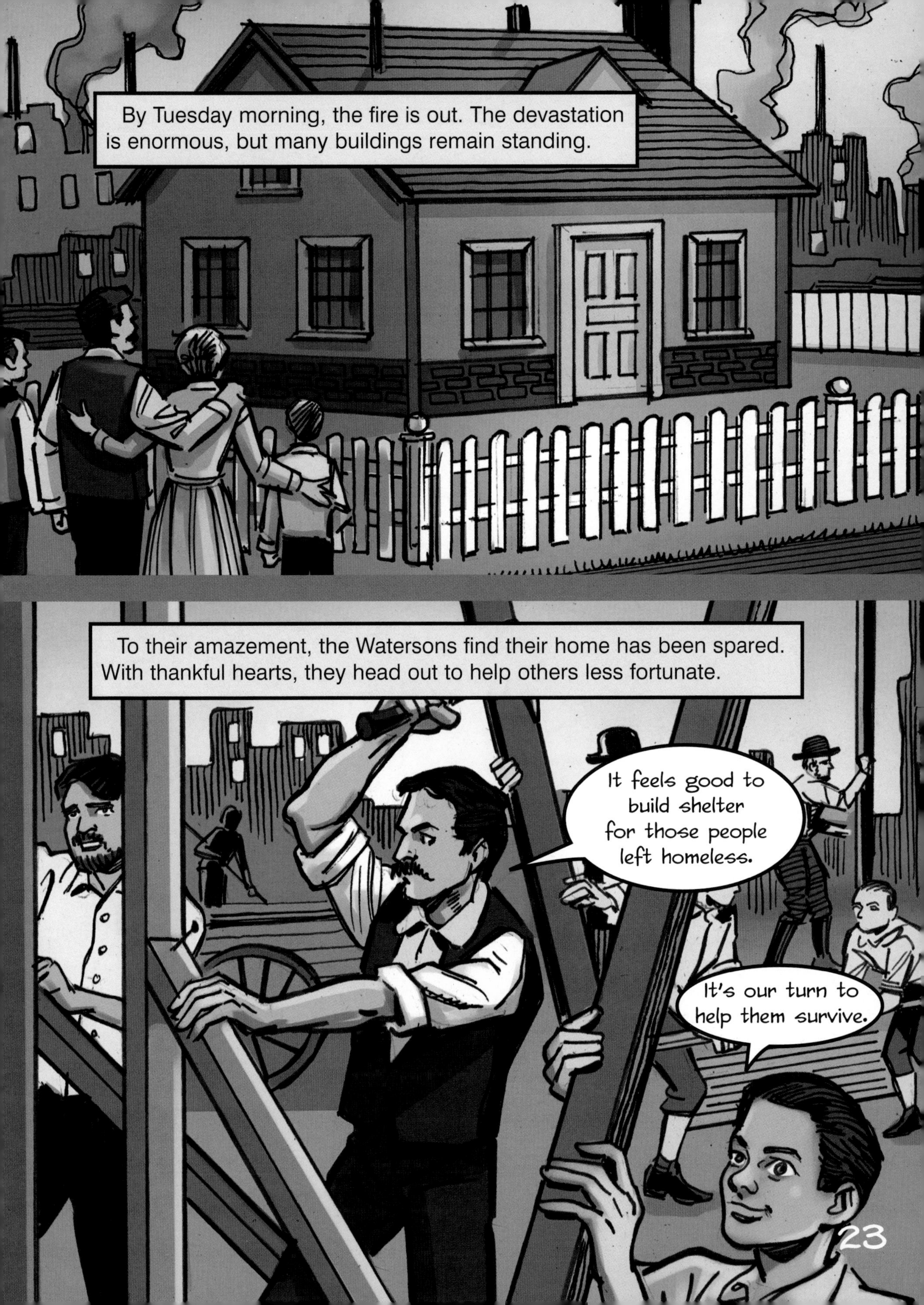
By Tuesday morning, the fire is out. The devastation is enormous, but many buildings remain standing.
To their amazement, the Watersons find their home has been spared. With thankful hearts, they head out to help others less fortunate.
It feels good to build shelter for those people left homeless.
It's our turn to help them survive.

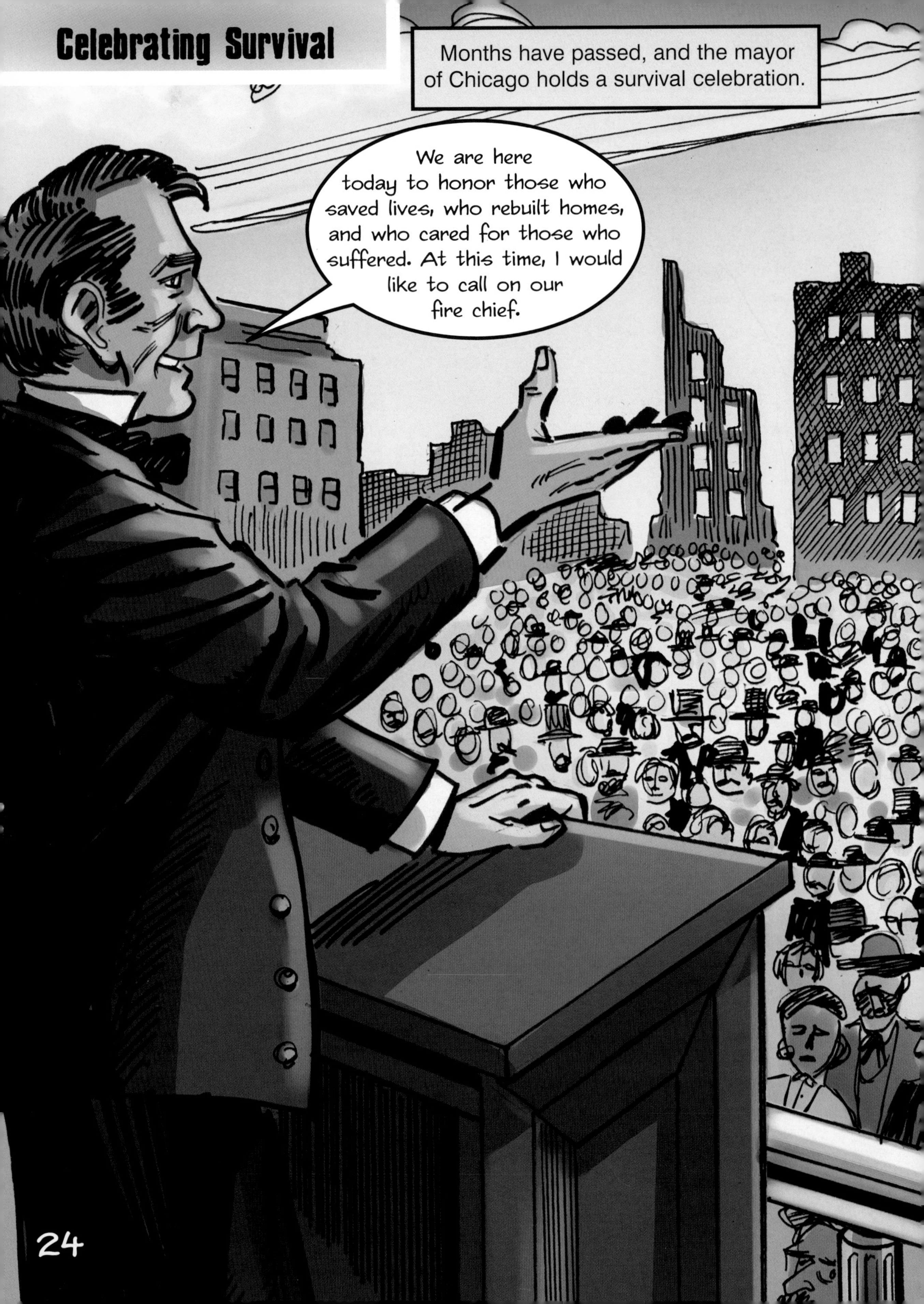
Months have passed, and the mayor of Chicago holds a survival celebration.
We are here today to honor those who saved lives, who rebuilt homes, and who cared for those who suffered. At this time, I would like to call on our fire chief.

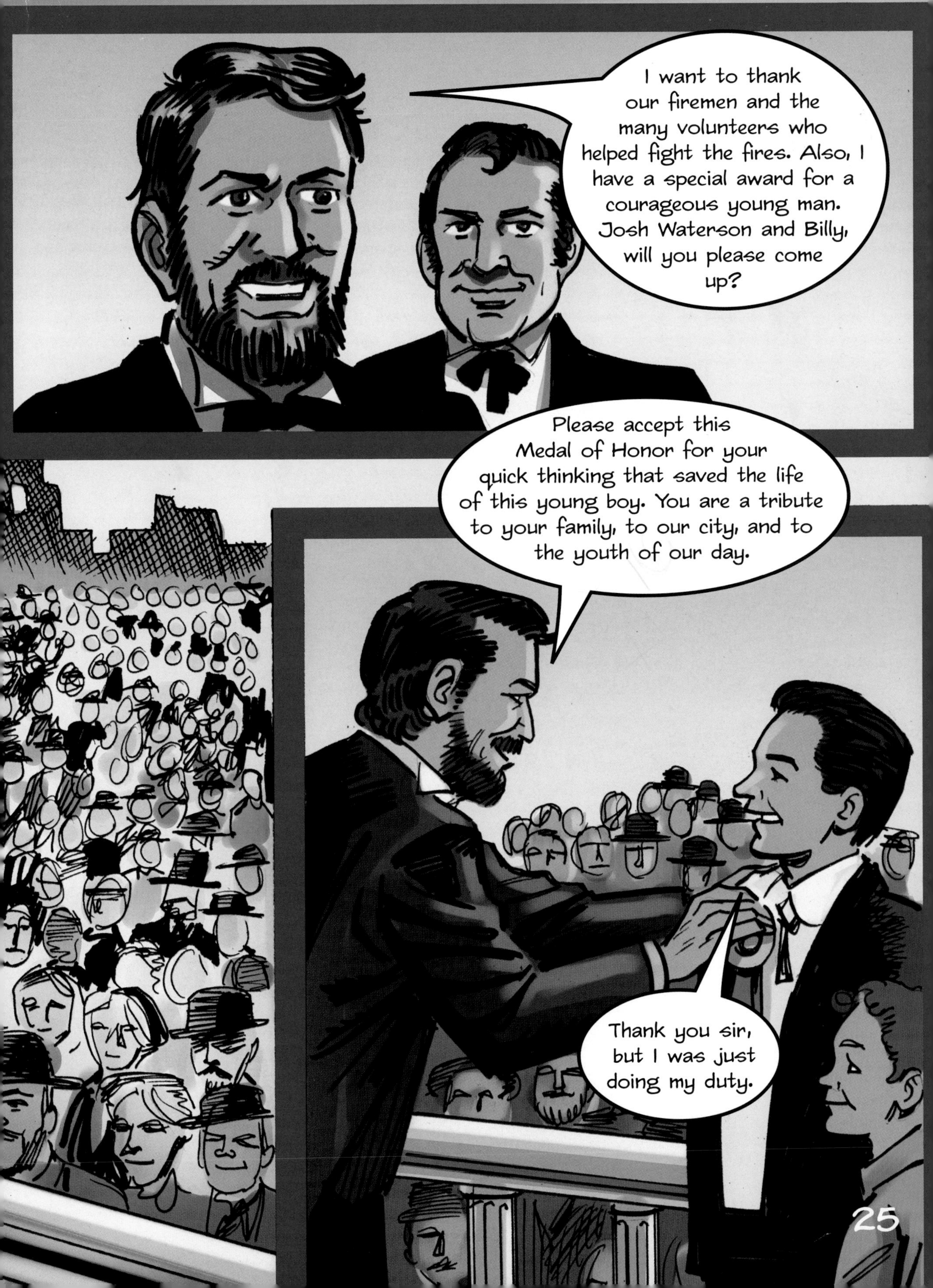
I want to thank our firemen and the many volunteers who helped fight the fires. Also, I have a special award for a courageous young man. Josh Waterson and Billy, will you please come up?
Please accept this Medal of Honor for your quick thinking that saved the life of this young boy. You are a tribute to your family, to our city, and to the youth of our day.
Thank you sir, but I was just doing my duty.

**What was the real cause of the Great Chicago Fire of 1871?**

No one knows for sure what really started the fire. One **legend** is that Mrs. O'Leary's cow kicked over a lantern inside the barn, which caught nearby straw on fire. It is true that flames were first seen

*Thousands ran to escape the intense heat and raging fires.*

near the O'Leary barn; however in 1911, the newspaper reporter who submitted that explanation admitted he made up the story.

The most accepted explanation seems well-founded. Mr. O'Leary told officials that on October 8, 1871, Mr. Daniel Sullivan came to Mr. O'Leary's door to alert the family that there was a fire in their barn. Decades later, just before he died, Mr. Sullivan confessed that he had sneaked into the O'Leary's barn to steal milk, and that he had started the fire.

Some scientists had an interesting idea. Two other fires broke out at exactly the same time in nearby cities. One was in Peshtigo, Wisconsin and another was in Holland, Michigan. They wondered if **splintering** comets might have set off all three fires.

Lake Michigan
Chicago River
Grant Park

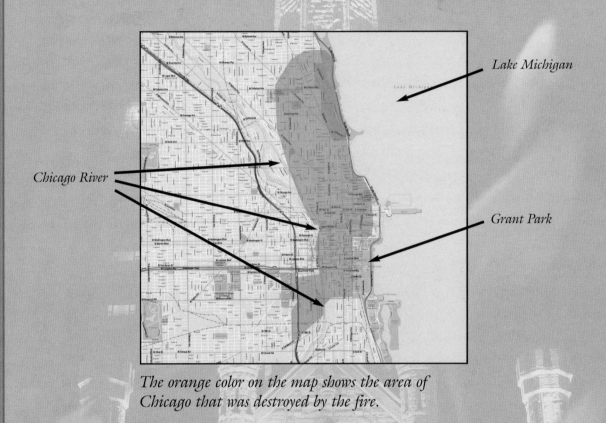

*The orange color on the map shows the area of Chicago that was destroyed by the fire.*

**In the 19th century, was it common for boys to take the same jobs as their fathers?**

Yes, most boys entered the same line of work as their fathers. They left school to become **apprentices** at their fathers' places of work to learn a trade or skill. Josh Waterson, the fictional character in this book, is still in school at age 16, which is unusual.

## How long did it take to rebuild Chicago?

Within four years, Chicago looked even better than it had before the Great Fire.

Workers began **reconstruction** immediately. They made temporary shelters for the homeless, repaired damaged buildings, constructed new city facilities, and fixed streets and railroad lines. Volunteers included both the young and the old, and the rich and the poor. There were people from the Chicago area and from other cities, and even prisoners whose lives were spared when their courthouse cells were unlocked.

City officials paid close attention to ways of preventing future fire disasters, by replacing wooden structures with stone, adding sprinkler systems, and installing other fire safeguards that were not present in 1871.

To this day, Chicago is one of the most visited cities in the United States.

*Parts of Grant Park are built upon debris from structures that burned during the fire.*

**What Would You See If You Visit Chicago Today?**

If you visit Chicago, there are lots of attractions for you to see, including areas where the fire occurred. The old Water Tower and Chicago Pumping Station are the only public buildings that were left standing after the fire. You can tour the tower and learn about its history. You might even get a glimpse of a ghost that is rumored to haunt the upstairs! Other places of interest include an architectural boat tour along the Chicago River, Lincoln Park and its free zoo, and Grant Park with all of its lovely gardens and walkways. When you get hungry, be sure to stop along the way and enjoy Chicago's world-famous hotdogs and deep-dish pizzas.

# Websites

www.americaslibrary.gov/cgi-bin/page.cgi/jb/
   recon/chicago_1

www.chicagohs.org/fire/intro/gcf-index.html

www.chicagohs.org/history/fire.html

en.wikipedia.org/wiki/Great_Chicago_Fire

# Glossary

**alert** (uh-LURT): An alert is a signal warning of danger.

**apprentices** (uh-PREN-tiss-ez): Apprentices are unpaid workers who work to learn a skill or job. Usually, they work beside someone who is already an expert to learn the necessary skills.

**devastation** (dev-uh-STAY-shuhn): Devastation is complete ruin.

**intense** (in-TENSS): If a fire is intense, it is very, very hot.

**legend** (LEJ-uhnd): A legend is a story that has been told many times over the years. It is often based on fact, but is not entirely a true story.

**panicky** (PAN-ik-ee): When people are panicky, they are so frightened they can't think straight.

**raging** (RAYJ-ing): A raging fire is very, very strong. It is so strong that it makes a roaring sound.

**reconstruction** (ree-kuhn-STRUHKT-shun): Reconstruction is the rebuilding of areas that have been destroyed. Workers repair or replace homes, schools, hotels, churches, stores, factories, and other buildings that have been damaged.

**smoldering** (SMOHL-dur-ing): Something is smoldering if it is still giving off smoke and heat after the flames of a fire have been put out.

**splintering** (SPLIN-tur-ing): If something starts splintering, it begins to break apart.

**stomped** (STOMPT): Slammed feet hard on the ground. If someone is stomped on by a horse, it ran right on top of that person.

**survive** (sur-VIVE): To survive is to live through a very dangerous time.

**timber** (TIM-bur): Timber is wood.

**watchtower** (WOCH-tou-ur): A watchtower is a tall building from which workers keep looking all the time for possible trouble. If a watchman sees a fire, he sends out a danger signal.

# Index

cause   26

courthouse   15, 16, 28

cow   26

devastation   21, 23

firefighters   12, 13

homeless   23, 28

Lake Michigan   5, 14, 20, 27

prisoners   15, 16, 28

rain(s)   22

rebuild   28

smoke   7, 14

volunteers   25, 28

water   14, 16, 17

waterworks   17

# About the Author

Jo Cleland, Professor Emeritus of Reading Education, taught in the College of Education at Arizona State University for 11 years. Prior to entering university teaching, Jo spent 20 years in public education and continues to work with children through her storytelling and workshops. She has presented to audiences of teachers and students across the nation and the world, bringing to all her favorite message: **what we learn with delight, we never forget**.

# About the Illustrator

Pete McDonnell is an illustrator who has worked in his field for twenty-four years. He has been creating comics, storyboards, and pop-art style illustration for clients such as Marvel Comics, the History Channel, Microsoft, Nestle, Sega, and many more. He lives in Sonoma County, California with his wife Shannon (also an illustrator) and son Jacob.